Office Automation Mastery

Transform Your Workplace with Cutting-Edge Tools and
Techniques

Casey Mendoza

1

Office Automation Mastery

Table of Contents

Chapter 1: Understanding Office Automation

Defining Office Automation

Office automation represents a transformative shift in the way businesses operate, streamlining processes and enhancing productivity through the integration of technology. At its core, office automation involves the use of various software and hardware solutions to perform routine tasks that were traditionally handled manually. This shift not only reduces the time and effort required to complete these tasks but also minimizes the potential for human error, leading to more efficient and reliable outcomes.

The concept of office automation is not new; it has evolved significantly over the decades. In the early days, automation was primarily associated with the mechanization of physical tasks, such as the use of typewriters and calculators. However, with the advent of computers and the internet, the scope of automation expanded dramatically. Today, office automation encompasses a wide range of activities, from managing emails and scheduling meetings to processing complex data and generating reports.

One of the key benefits of office automation is the ability to free up valuable time for employees, allowing them to focus on more strategic and creative tasks. By automating repetitive and mundane activities, businesses can enhance their overall productivity and foster a more innovative work environment. This shift not only improves the efficiency of individual employees but also contributes to the organization's success as a whole.

Moreover, office automation facilitates better communication and collaboration within teams. With tools that enable seamless sharing of information and real-time collaboration, employees can work together more effectively, regardless of their physical location. This is particularly important in today's globalized world, where remote work and virtual teams are becoming increasingly common.

Despite its numerous advantages, office automation is often misunderstood. Some people fear that automation will lead to job losses, as machines and software take over tasks traditionally performed by humans. However, this perspective overlooks the potential for automation to create new opportunities and roles within organizations. Rather than replacing human workers, automation can augment their capabilities, enabling them to take on more complex and rewarding tasks.

Another common misconception is that office automation is only relevant for large corporations with substantial resources. In reality, businesses of all sizes can benefit from automation, as there are solutions available to suit a wide range of needs and budgets. Small and medium-sized enterprises, in particular, can leverage automation to level the playing field and compete more effectively with larger competitors.

As technology continues to advance, the future of office automation looks promising. Emerging trends, such as the integration of artificial intelligence and machine learning, are set to further enhance the capabilities of automation tools. These technologies can analyze vast amounts of data and provide valuable insights, enabling businesses to make more informed decisions and optimize their operations.

In addition, the increasing prevalence of cloud-based solutions is making office automation more accessible and affordable than ever before. With cloud technology, businesses can access powerful automation tools without the need for significant upfront investments in hardware or infrastructure. This democratization of technology is empowering organizations of all sizes to harness the benefits of automation and drive their growth.

To fully realize the potential of office automation, it is essential for businesses to adopt a strategic approach. This involves carefully assessing their current processes and identifying areas where automation can have the greatest impact. By prioritizing tasks that are time-consuming, repetitive, or prone to error, organizations can maximize the benefits of automation and achieve a higher return on investment.

Furthermore, successful implementation of office automation requires a commitment to continuous improvement. As technology evolves and new tools become available, businesses must be willing to adapt and refine their automation strategies. This may involve regularly reviewing and updating their processes, as well as investing in training and development to ensure that employees have the skills and knowledge needed to work effectively with automated systems.

In conclusion, office automation is a powerful tool that can transform the way businesses operate, enhancing productivity, efficiency, and collaboration. By understanding the true potential of automation and embracing it strategically, organizations can unlock new opportunities and drive their success in an increasingly competitive landscape.

Historical Context and Evolution

The journey of office automation is a fascinating tale of technological evolution, marked by significant milestones that have reshaped the way businesses operate. To understand its historical context, one must first appreciate the early days of office work, where manual processes dominated the landscape. In the late 19th and early 20th centuries, offices were bustling with clerks and typists, each performing tasks that required meticulous attention to detail. The introduction of the typewriter in the 1860s marked one of the first steps towards mechanization, revolutionizing the way documents were produced and setting the stage for future innovations.

As the 20th century progressed, the demand for efficiency and productivity in the workplace grew. The invention of the telephone and the telegraph transformed communication, allowing businesses to connect with clients and partners across great distances. These technologies laid the groundwork for a more interconnected world, where information could be exchanged rapidly and efficiently. The development of the photocopier in the mid-20th century further streamlined office operations, enabling the quick duplication of documents and reducing the reliance on manual copying.

The real turning point in office automation came with the advent of computers. In the 1960s and 1970s, computers began to make their way into the business world, initially as large, room-sized machines used primarily for data processing. These early computers were expensive and complex, accessible only to large corporations with the resources to invest in such technology. However, they demonstrated the potential of automation to handle repetitive tasks with speed and accuracy, paving the way for more widespread adoption.

The personal computer revolution of the 1980s brought computing power to the masses, transforming the office environment once again. With the introduction of user-friendly software applications, such as word processors and spreadsheets, employees could perform a wide range of tasks more efficiently than ever before. This democratization of technology allowed businesses of all sizes to benefit from automation, leveling the playing field and fostering innovation.

The rise of the internet in the 1990s marked another significant milestone in the evolution of office automation. The ability to connect computers across the globe opened up new possibilities for collaboration and information sharing. Email became a ubiquitous tool for communication, replacing traditional mail and enabling instant exchanges of information. The internet also facilitated the development of cloud-based solutions, allowing businesses to access powerful software applications without the need for costly infrastructure.

As the 21st century unfolded, the pace of technological advancement accelerated. Mobile devices, such as smartphones and tablets, brought unprecedented flexibility to the workplace, enabling employees to work from virtually anywhere. This shift towards mobility and remote work further emphasized the importance of automation in maintaining productivity and efficiency. Businesses began to adopt a wide range of tools and platforms designed to streamline processes, from project management software to customer relationship management systems.

Throughout this journey, the role of office automation has continually evolved, adapting to the changing needs of businesses and the technological landscape. Today, automation is an integral part of the modern workplace, driving innovation and enabling organizations to operate more efficiently and effectively. The historical context of office automation is a testament to the power of technology to transform the way we work, offering valuable lessons for businesses seeking to harness its potential.

Understanding this evolution provides valuable insights into the future of office automation. As technology continues to advance, new opportunities and challenges will emerge, requiring businesses to remain agile and adaptable. By learning from the past and embracing the possibilities of the present, organizations can position themselves for success in an increasingly automated world. The journey of office automation is far from over, and its future promises to be as dynamic and transformative as its past.

Key Benefits of Automation

Automation has become a cornerstone of modern business operations, offering a multitude of benefits that extend beyond mere efficiency. At its core, automation is about leveraging technology to perform tasks that were once manual, repetitive, and time-consuming. This shift not only enhances productivity but also opens up new avenues for innovation and growth. Understanding the key benefits of automation can help businesses make informed decisions about integrating these technologies into their operations.

One of the most significant advantages of automation is the dramatic increase in efficiency it provides. By automating routine tasks, businesses can significantly reduce the time and effort required to complete them. This efficiency gain allows employees to focus on more strategic and creative endeavors, ultimately driving the organization forward. For instance, automating data entry processes can free up valuable time for employees to analyze and interpret data, leading to more informed decision-making.

In addition to efficiency, automation also enhances accuracy and consistency. Human error is an inherent risk in manual processes, particularly when dealing with large volumes of data or complex calculations. Automation minimizes this risk by ensuring that tasks are performed with precision and uniformity. This consistency is particularly valuable in industries where compliance and quality control are critical, such as healthcare and finance. By reducing errors, businesses can improve their overall quality of service and build trust with their clients and partners.

Cost savings are another compelling benefit of automation. While the initial investment in automation technology can be significant, the long-term savings often outweigh these costs. By reducing the need for manual labor and minimizing errors, businesses can lower their operational expenses and improve their bottom line. Moreover, automation can lead to increased output without a corresponding increase in labor costs, allowing businesses to scale more effectively.

Automation also plays a crucial role in enhancing customer satisfaction. In today's fast-paced world, customers expect quick and efficient service. Automation enables businesses to meet these expectations by streamlining processes and reducing response times. For example, automated customer service systems can handle routine inquiries and support requests, freeing up human agents to address more complex issues. This not only improves the customer experience but also allows businesses to serve a larger customer base without compromising quality.

Another key benefit of automation is its ability to facilitate better decision-making. By automating data collection and analysis, businesses can gain valuable insights into their operations and market trends. This data-driven approach enables organizations to make more informed decisions, identify opportunities for improvement, and respond more effectively to changing market conditions. Automation tools can also provide real-time analytics and reporting, allowing businesses to monitor their performance and make adjustments as needed.

Furthermore, automation fosters innovation by freeing up resources and encouraging a culture of continuous improvement. When employees are relieved of repetitive tasks, they have more time and energy to devote to creative problem-solving and strategic initiatives. This shift can lead to the development of new products, services, and business models, driving growth and competitiveness. By embracing automation, businesses can create an environment that encourages experimentation and innovation, ultimately leading to greater success.

Scalability is another important advantage of automation. As businesses grow, the demands on their operations increase. Automation allows organizations to scale their processes without a proportional increase in resources. This scalability is particularly valuable for businesses looking to expand into new markets or increase their production capacity. By automating key processes, businesses can ensure that their operations remain efficient and effective, even as they grow.

Finally, automation can enhance employee satisfaction and engagement. By eliminating mundane and repetitive tasks, automation allows employees to focus on more meaningful and fulfilling work. This shift can lead to increased job satisfaction, higher morale, and reduced turnover. Moreover, automation can provide employees with opportunities to develop new skills and take on more challenging roles, further enhancing their engagement and commitment to the organization.

In conclusion, the key benefits of automation extend far beyond efficiency and cost savings. By enhancing accuracy, improving customer satisfaction, facilitating better decision-making, fostering innovation, enabling scalability, and boosting employee engagement, automation can transform the way businesses operate and compete in the modern world. Understanding these benefits is essential for organizations looking to harness the power of automation and drive their success in an increasingly competitive landscape.

Common Misconceptions

Misconceptions about automation abound, often clouding judgment and hindering progress. These misunderstandings can create barriers to adoption, leading to missed opportunities and inefficiencies. By addressing these misconceptions, businesses can make more informed decisions and fully leverage the benefits of automation.

One prevalent misconception is that automation leads to widespread job loss. While it's true that automation can replace certain tasks, it doesn't necessarily equate to a reduction in overall employment. Instead, automation often transforms jobs, shifting the focus from repetitive tasks to more strategic and creative roles. This evolution can lead to the creation of new job opportunities that require different skill sets. For example, as routine data entry tasks become automated, employees can transition to roles that involve data analysis and interpretation, adding value to the organization.

Another common misunderstanding is that automation is only suitable for large enterprises with substantial resources. In reality, automation technologies have become increasingly accessible and affordable, making them viable options for businesses of all sizes. Small and medium-sized enterprises (SMEs) can benefit from automation by streamlining their operations, reducing costs, and improving efficiency. Cloud-based solutions and software-as-a-service (SaaS) models have further democratized access to automation tools, allowing businesses to implement them without significant upfront investments.

There's also a misconception that automation is a one-size-fits-all solution. In truth, successful automation requires a tailored approach that considers the unique needs and goals of each organization. Businesses must carefully assess their processes to identify areas where automation can provide the most value. This involves understanding the specific challenges and opportunities within their operations and selecting the right tools and technologies to address them. Customization and flexibility are key to ensuring that automation initiatives align with business objectives and deliver the desired outcomes.

Some believe that automation is synonymous with complexity and requires extensive technical expertise to implement and manage. While certain automation solutions can be complex, many modern tools are designed with user-friendliness in mind. These solutions often feature intuitive interfaces and offer comprehensive support and training resources to help businesses get started. Additionally, partnering with experienced vendors or consultants can provide valuable guidance and expertise, simplifying the implementation process and ensuring a smooth transition.

A further misconception is that automation eliminates the need for human oversight and intervention. While automation can handle many tasks independently, human involvement remains crucial for monitoring, decision-making, and problem-solving. Automation should be viewed as a tool that complements human capabilities, enhancing productivity and efficiency rather than replacing human input entirely. By maintaining a balance between automation and human oversight, businesses can ensure that their operations remain agile and responsive to changing conditions.

There's also a tendency to view automation as a purely technical endeavor, disconnected from broader business strategy. In reality, automation should be integrated into the overall strategic framework of the organization. This involves aligning automation initiatives with business goals, ensuring that they support and enhance the company's mission and vision. By taking a strategic approach to automation, businesses can maximize its impact and drive long-term success.

Another misconception is that automation is a static, one-time implementation. In fact, automation is an ongoing process that requires continuous evaluation and adaptation. As technology evolves and business needs change, automation solutions must be regularly assessed and updated to remain effective. This dynamic approach ensures that automation continues to deliver value and supports the organization's growth and development.

Some may also believe that automation stifles creativity and innovation by imposing rigid processes and structures. On the contrary, automation can free up time and resources, allowing employees to focus on creative problem-solving and strategic initiatives. By automating routine tasks, businesses can foster a culture of innovation, encouraging employees to explore new ideas and approaches. This shift can lead to the development of innovative products, services, and business models, driving competitiveness and growth.

Finally, there's a misconception that automation is solely about cost reduction. While cost savings are a significant benefit, automation offers a wide range of advantages beyond financial considerations. These include improved accuracy, enhanced customer satisfaction, better decision-making, and increased scalability. By recognizing the full spectrum of benefits that automation can provide, businesses can make more informed decisions and fully leverage its potential.

Addressing these common misconceptions is essential for businesses looking to harness the power of automation. By dispelling these myths and gaining a clearer understanding of what automation entails, organizations can make more informed decisions and implement solutions that align with their goals and objectives. This clarity can pave the way for successful automation initiatives that drive efficiency, innovation, and growth.

Future Trends in Office Automation

The landscape of office automation is rapidly evolving, driven by technological advancements and changing workplace dynamics. As businesses strive to enhance productivity and efficiency, understanding future trends in office automation becomes crucial. These trends not only shape the way organizations operate but also redefine the roles of employees and the nature of work itself.

One significant trend is the increasing integration of cloud-based solutions. Cloud technology offers unparalleled flexibility and scalability, enabling businesses to access and manage their data and applications from anywhere, at any time. This shift towards cloud-based platforms facilitates remote work, a trend that has gained momentum in recent years. By leveraging cloud technology, organizations can ensure seamless collaboration and communication among team members, regardless of their physical location. This trend is likely to continue as businesses recognize the benefits of a distributed workforce and the potential for cost savings on physical office space.

Another emerging trend is the rise of smart office technologies. These innovations aim to create more efficient and comfortable work environments by utilizing the Internet of Things (IoT) and data analytics. Smart office solutions can optimize energy consumption, enhance security, and improve employee well-being. For instance, IoT-enabled devices can adjust lighting and temperature based on occupancy and preferences, creating a more conducive work environment. Additionally, data analytics can provide insights into space utilization and employee productivity, allowing organizations to make informed decisions about office design and resource allocation.

The growing emphasis on data-driven decision-making is also shaping the future of office automation. As businesses collect and analyze vast amounts of data, they can gain valuable insights into their operations and customer behavior. This data-driven approach enables organizations to make more informed decisions, optimize processes, and identify new opportunities for growth. Automation tools that incorporate advanced analytics and machine learning algorithms can help businesses harness the power of data, transforming raw information into actionable insights.

Collaboration tools are evolving to meet the demands of modern workplaces. As teams become more diverse and geographically dispersed, effective collaboration becomes essential. Future trends in office automation include the development of more sophisticated collaboration platforms that integrate various communication channels, such as video conferencing, instant messaging, and project management tools. These platforms aim to streamline communication and foster a sense of community among team members, regardless of their location. By enhancing collaboration, businesses can improve productivity and drive innovation.

The focus on employee experience is another trend shaping office automation. As organizations recognize the importance of employee satisfaction and engagement, they are investing in technologies that enhance the overall work experience. Automation tools that simplify routine tasks and reduce administrative burdens can free up employees' time, allowing them to focus on more meaningful and fulfilling work. Additionally, personalized learning and development platforms can help employees acquire new skills and advance their careers, contributing to a more motivated and engaged workforce.

Security and privacy concerns are becoming increasingly important in the realm of office automation. As businesses adopt more digital tools and platforms, they must ensure that their data and systems are protected from cyber threats. Future trends in office automation include the development of more robust security measures, such as advanced encryption techniques and multi-factor authentication. By prioritizing security and privacy, organizations can safeguard their sensitive information and maintain the trust of their employees and customers.

The concept of the paperless office is gaining traction as businesses seek to reduce their environmental impact and streamline operations. Digital document management systems and electronic signatures are becoming more prevalent, enabling organizations to eliminate paper-based processes and improve efficiency. This trend not only supports sustainability initiatives but also enhances document accessibility and collaboration. As businesses continue to embrace digital transformation, the paperless office is likely to become a standard practice.

The role of artificial intelligence (AI) in office automation is expanding, with AI-powered tools becoming more sophisticated and capable. These tools can automate complex tasks, such as data analysis and customer service, freeing up employees to focus on higher-value activities. AI can also enhance decision-making by providing predictive insights and recommendations based on historical data. As AI technology continues to advance, its applications in office automation are expected to grow, offering new opportunities for innovation and efficiency.

The future of office automation is also influenced by the increasing importance of sustainability and corporate social responsibility. Businesses are recognizing the need to adopt environmentally friendly practices and contribute to the well-being of their communities. Automation technologies that support sustainability, such as energy-efficient systems and waste reduction solutions, are becoming more prevalent. By aligning their automation strategies with sustainability goals, organizations can enhance their reputation and create long-term value for their stakeholders.

As the workplace continues to evolve, the role of office automation will become increasingly integral to business success. By staying informed about future trends and embracing new technologies, organizations can position themselves for growth and innovation. These trends not only enhance operational efficiency but also create more dynamic and fulfilling work environments, ultimately driving competitiveness and success in the modern business landscape.

Chapter 2: Essential Tools for Office Automation

Email Management Tools

Email management tools have become indispensable in today's fast-paced digital world, where the volume of emails can be overwhelming. For beginners, navigating the myriad of options available can be daunting, but understanding the core functionalities and benefits of these tools can significantly enhance productivity and organization.

The primary function of email management tools is to streamline the process of handling emails, making it more efficient and less time-consuming. One of the most common features is the ability to categorize and prioritize emails. By automatically sorting incoming messages into folders based on predefined criteria, such as sender or subject, users can quickly identify which emails require immediate attention and which can be addressed later. This categorization helps prevent important messages from getting lost in the clutter of a crowded inbox.

Another valuable feature is the ability to schedule emails. Many email management tools allow users to compose messages and set a specific time for them to be sent. This is particularly useful for professionals who work across different time zones or need to send reminders and follow-ups at optimal times. By scheduling emails, users can ensure that their messages are delivered when they are most likely to be read and acted upon.

Email management tools often include advanced search capabilities, enabling users to locate specific emails quickly.

With the ability to search by keywords, dates, or attachments, users can retrieve important information without sifting through countless messages. This feature is especially beneficial for those who need to reference past communications or gather data for reports and presentations.

For those who struggle with managing multiple email accounts, consolidation features can be a game-changer. Many tools offer the ability to integrate various email accounts into a single interface, allowing users to manage all their communications from one place. This not only saves time but also reduces the likelihood of missing important messages from different accounts.

Automation is another key aspect of email management tools. By setting up rules and filters, users can automate repetitive tasks, such as archiving old emails or forwarding messages to specific team members. Automation reduces the manual effort required to maintain an organized inbox and ensures that important tasks are not overlooked.

Security is a critical consideration when choosing an email management tool. With the increasing prevalence of cyber threats, it's essential to select a tool that offers robust security features, such as encryption and spam filtering. These features protect sensitive information and prevent unauthorized access to email accounts.

Collaboration is an integral part of modern work environments, and many email management tools offer features that facilitate teamwork. Shared inboxes, for example, allow multiple users to access and manage emails from a single account, making it easier to collaborate on projects and respond to customer inquiries. Additionally, some tools offer integration with other productivity apps, such as calendars and task managers, to streamline workflows and enhance team coordination.

Customization is another advantage of email management tools. Users can tailor the interface and functionalities to suit their preferences and work habits. Whether it's adjusting the layout, setting up custom notifications, or creating personalized templates, customization options allow users to create an email management system that aligns with their unique needs.

For beginners, the learning curve associated with email management tools can be a concern. However, many tools offer user-friendly interfaces and provide tutorials and support to help users get started. By investing a little time in learning how to use these tools effectively, beginners can reap significant benefits in terms of productivity and organization.

The integration of artificial intelligence and machine learning into email management tools is an emerging trend that promises to further enhance their capabilities. These technologies can analyze user behavior and preferences to provide personalized recommendations and automate complex tasks. While this trend is still in its early stages, it holds great potential for transforming the way we manage emails.

Choosing the right email management tool depends on individual needs and preferences. Factors to consider include the size of the organization, the volume of emails, and the specific features required. It's important to evaluate different options and take advantage of free trials to determine which tool best meets one's needs.

Email management tools offer a range of features designed to enhance productivity, organization, and security. By understanding and leveraging these tools, beginners can take control of their inboxes and improve their overall efficiency. As technology continues to evolve, the capabilities of email management tools will only expand, offering even more opportunities for optimization and innovation.

Project Management Software

Project management software has revolutionized the way teams collaborate and execute tasks, offering a structured approach to managing projects of varying complexity. For beginners, understanding the core functionalities and benefits of these tools is essential to harnessing their full potential.

At the heart of project management software lies the ability to organize tasks and resources efficiently. These tools provide a centralized platform where team members can create, assign, and track tasks, ensuring that everyone is aligned with the project's objectives. By breaking down projects into manageable tasks, teams can focus on specific goals and monitor progress in real-time. This granular approach not only enhances accountability but also facilitates timely completion of tasks.

One of the standout features of project management software is the visual representation of project timelines. Gantt charts, for instance, offer a graphical depiction of a project's schedule, illustrating the start and end dates of tasks, dependencies, and milestones. This visual aid helps teams identify potential bottlenecks and allocate resources effectively, ensuring that projects stay on track. For beginners, the ability to visualize the entire project lifecycle can be invaluable in understanding how individual tasks contribute to the overall success of the project.

Collaboration is a cornerstone of successful project management, and these tools are designed to foster seamless communication among team members. Features such as shared workspaces, discussion boards, and file-sharing capabilities enable teams to collaborate in real-time, regardless of geographical location. This connectivity ensures that team members can share updates, provide feedback, and resolve issues promptly, reducing the risk of miscommunication and delays.

Resource management is another critical aspect of project management software. By providing insights into resource allocation and availability, these tools help project managers optimize the use of personnel, equipment, and budget. This ensures that resources are not overextended and that projects are executed within the constraints of time and cost. For beginners, understanding resource management is key to preventing burnout and ensuring sustainable project execution.

Risk management is an often-overlooked component of project management, yet it is crucial for mitigating potential challenges. Project management software offers tools for identifying, assessing, and monitoring risks throughout the project lifecycle. By proactively addressing potential issues, teams can develop contingency plans and minimize the impact of unforeseen events. This proactive approach to risk management is essential for maintaining project momentum and achieving desired outcomes.

Customization is a significant advantage of project management software, allowing teams to tailor the platform to their specific needs. Whether it's customizing dashboards, creating personalized workflows, or setting up automated notifications, these tools offer flexibility to accommodate diverse project requirements. For beginners, the ability to customize the software ensures that it aligns with their unique work processes and enhances overall productivity.

Integration with other tools and applications is a feature that enhances the functionality of project management software. By connecting with tools such as email, calendars, and customer relationship management systems, teams can streamline workflows and reduce the need for manual data entry. This integration not only saves time but also ensures that information is consistent and up-to-date across all platforms.

For beginners, the learning curve associated with project management software can be a concern. However, many tools offer intuitive interfaces and provide tutorials, webinars, and support to help users get started. By investing time in learning how to use these tools effectively, beginners can unlock significant benefits in terms of efficiency and collaboration.

Security is a paramount consideration when selecting project management software. With sensitive project data and proprietary information at stake, it's essential to choose a tool that offers robust security features, such as encryption, access controls, and regular backups. These measures protect against data breaches and ensure that project information remains confidential and secure.

Choosing the right project management software depends on various factors, including the size of the team, the complexity of projects, and the specific features required. It's important to evaluate different options and take advantage of free trials to determine which tool best meets one's needs. By selecting the right software, teams can enhance their project management capabilities and achieve their goals more efficiently.

Project management software offers a comprehensive suite of features designed to enhance collaboration, organization, and efficiency. By understanding and leveraging these tools, beginners can take control of their projects and improve their overall productivity. As technology continues to evolve, the capabilities of project management software will only expand, offering even more opportunities for optimization and innovation.

Document Automation Solutions

Document automation solutions have emerged as a transformative force in the realm of business operations, offering a streamlined approach to managing and processing documents. For beginners, understanding the intricacies of these solutions is crucial to leveraging their full potential and enhancing organizational efficiency.

At the core of document automation lies the ability to automate repetitive and time-consuming tasks associated with document creation, management, and distribution. By utilizing predefined templates and workflows, these solutions enable users to generate documents with minimal manual intervention. This not only reduces the likelihood of errors but also accelerates the document creation process, allowing teams to focus on more strategic activities.

One of the primary benefits of document automation solutions is the consistency they bring to document formatting and content. By standardizing templates, organizations can ensure that all documents adhere to brand guidelines and regulatory requirements. This uniformity is particularly important in industries where compliance is critical, such as finance and healthcare. For beginners, the assurance that documents are consistently formatted and compliant can significantly reduce the stress associated with document management.

Collaboration is a key aspect of document automation solutions, as they facilitate seamless communication and coordination among team members. Features such as version control, real-time editing, and commenting capabilities enable multiple users to work on a document simultaneously, ensuring that everyone is on the same page. This collaborative environment not only enhances productivity but also fosters a sense of teamwork and shared responsibility.

Integration with existing systems and applications is a hallmark of effective document automation solutions. By connecting with tools such as customer relationship management (CRM) systems, enterprise resource planning (ERP) software, and cloud storage platforms, these solutions enable organizations to streamline workflows and eliminate data silos. This integration ensures that information is consistent and accessible across all platforms, reducing the need for manual data entry and minimizing the risk of errors.

Security is a paramount consideration when implementing document automation solutions. With sensitive information often contained within documents, it's essential to choose a solution that offers robust security features, such as encryption, access controls, and audit trails. These measures protect against unauthorized access and ensure that document integrity is maintained. For beginners, understanding the importance of security in document automation is crucial to safeguarding organizational data.

Customization is another significant advantage of document automation solutions, allowing organizations to tailor the platform to their specific needs. Whether it's customizing templates, creating personalized workflows, or setting up automated notifications, these solutions offer flexibility to accommodate diverse business requirements. For beginners, the ability to customize the software ensures that it aligns with their unique work processes and enhances overall productivity.

The learning curve associated with document automation solutions can be a concern for beginners. However, many tools offer intuitive interfaces and provide tutorials, webinars, and support to help users get started. By investing time in learning how to use these tools effectively, beginners can unlock significant benefits in terms of efficiency and collaboration.

Cost savings are a tangible benefit of document automation solutions, as they reduce the need for manual labor and minimize the risk of errors. By automating document-related tasks, organizations can allocate resources more effectively and reduce operational costs. This financial advantage is particularly appealing to small businesses and startups looking to optimize their operations without incurring significant expenses.

Scalability is a critical consideration for organizations looking to implement document automation solutions. As businesses grow and evolve, their document management needs may change. Choosing a solution that can scale with the organization ensures that it remains relevant and effective over time. For beginners, understanding the importance of scalability is key to selecting a solution that will support long-term growth and success.

Document automation solutions offer a comprehensive suite of features designed to enhance efficiency, consistency, and collaboration. By understanding and leveraging these tools, beginners can take control of their document management processes and improve their overall productivity. As technology continues to evolve, the capabilities of document automation solutions will only expand, offering even more opportunities for optimization and innovation.

Customer Relationship Management (CRM) Systems

Customer Relationship Management (CRM) systems have become indispensable tools for businesses seeking to cultivate and maintain strong relationships with their customers. These systems offer a centralized platform for managing interactions, tracking customer data, and streamlining communication, ultimately enhancing customer satisfaction and loyalty. For beginners, understanding the fundamental components and benefits of CRM systems is crucial to harnessing their full potential.

At the heart of any CRM system is the ability to consolidate customer information into a single, accessible database. This centralization allows businesses to maintain comprehensive records of customer interactions, preferences, and purchase history. By having a holistic view of each customer, businesses can tailor their marketing efforts and provide personalized experiences that resonate with individual needs. For beginners, the ability to access detailed customer profiles can significantly enhance the quality of customer interactions and improve overall service delivery.

One of the primary advantages of CRM systems is their capacity to automate routine tasks and processes. From sending follow-up emails to scheduling appointments, CRM systems can handle a wide range of administrative tasks, freeing up valuable time for sales and customer service teams. This automation not only increases efficiency but also reduces the likelihood of human error, ensuring that customers receive timely and accurate information. For beginners, leveraging automation features can lead to more productive workdays and improved customer satisfaction.

CRM systems also play a pivotal role in facilitating communication and collaboration among team members. By providing a shared platform for accessing customer data and tracking interactions, CRM systems enable teams to work cohesively and stay informed about customer needs and preferences. This collaborative environment fosters a sense of teamwork and ensures that all team members are aligned in their efforts to deliver exceptional customer service. For beginners, the ability to collaborate effectively can lead to more successful customer interactions and stronger relationships.

Integration with other business tools and applications is a key feature of CRM systems. By connecting with email platforms, marketing automation tools, and e-commerce systems, CRM systems enable businesses to streamline workflows and ensure that customer data is consistent across all channels. This integration reduces the need for manual data entry and minimizes the risk of discrepancies, allowing businesses to maintain accurate and up-to-date customer records. For beginners, understanding the importance of integration can lead to more efficient and effective use of CRM systems.

Data analysis and reporting capabilities are essential components of CRM systems, providing businesses with valuable insights into customer behavior and preferences. By analyzing data such as purchase history, engagement metrics, and feedback, businesses can identify trends and patterns that inform strategic decision-making. These insights enable businesses to refine their marketing strategies, optimize sales processes, and enhance customer experiences. For beginners, the ability to access and interpret data can lead to more informed decisions and improved business outcomes.

Security is a critical consideration when implementing CRM systems, as they often contain sensitive customer information. It's essential to choose a CRM system that offers robust security features, such as encryption, access controls, and regular security updates. These measures protect against unauthorized access and ensure that customer data is safeguarded. For beginners, understanding the importance of security in CRM systems is crucial to maintaining customer trust and compliance with data protection regulations.

Customization is another significant advantage of CRM systems, allowing businesses to tailor the platform to their specific needs and workflows. Whether it's customizing dashboards, creating personalized reports, or setting up automated workflows, CRM systems offer flexibility to accommodate diverse business requirements. For beginners, the ability to customize the software ensures that it aligns with their unique work processes and enhances overall productivity.

The learning curve associated with CRM systems can be a concern for beginners. However, many CRM providers offer user-friendly interfaces and provide resources such as tutorials, webinars, and customer support to help users get started. By investing time in learning how to use these tools effectively, beginners can unlock significant benefits in terms of efficiency and customer relationship management.

Cost savings are a tangible benefit of CRM systems, as they reduce the need for manual labor and minimize the risk of errors. By automating customer-related tasks and streamlining processes, businesses can allocate resources more effectively and reduce operational costs. This financial advantage is particularly appealing to small businesses and startups looking to optimize their operations without incurring significant expenses.

Scalability is a critical consideration for businesses looking to implement CRM systems. As businesses grow and evolve, their customer relationship management needs may change. Choosing a CRM system that can scale with the organization ensures that it remains relevant and effective over time. For beginners, understanding the importance of scalability is key to selecting a solution that will support long-term growth and success.

CRM systems offer a comprehensive suite of features designed to enhance customer relationship management, streamline processes, and improve overall business performance. By understanding and leveraging these tools, beginners can take control of their customer interactions and build stronger, more meaningful relationships. As technology continues to evolve, the capabilities of CRM systems will only expand, offering even more opportunities for optimization and innovation.

Communication and Collaboration Tools

Communication and collaboration tools have revolutionized the way individuals and teams interact, breaking down geographical barriers and enabling seamless cooperation across diverse locations. These tools are essential for businesses, educational institutions, and even social groups, facilitating real-time communication, project management, and information sharing. For beginners, understanding the various types of tools available and how to effectively utilize them can significantly enhance productivity and foster a collaborative environment.

The digital age has ushered in a plethora of communication tools designed to cater to different needs and preferences. Instant messaging platforms, such as Slack and Microsoft Teams, offer a dynamic way to communicate quickly and efficiently. These platforms allow users to create channels for specific topics or projects, ensuring that conversations remain organized and relevant. The ability to send direct messages, share files, and integrate with other applications makes instant messaging an indispensable tool for modern communication. For beginners, mastering these platforms can lead to more effective and streamlined communication within teams.

Video conferencing tools have become increasingly popular, especially in the wake of remote work and virtual meetings. Platforms like Zoom, Google Meet, and Skype provide users with the ability to conduct face-to-face meetings without the need for physical presence. These tools offer features such as screen sharing, recording, and breakout rooms, enhancing the overall meeting experience. For beginners, understanding how to navigate and utilize video conferencing tools can lead to more engaging and productive virtual interactions.

Email remains a staple communication tool, offering a formal and reliable method for exchanging information. Despite the rise of instant messaging and video conferencing, email continues to be an essential tool for professional communication. It provides a written record of conversations, making it ideal for sharing detailed information, sending attachments, and maintaining a history of correspondence. For beginners, mastering email etiquette and organization can lead to more effective communication and a professional online presence.

Collaboration tools extend beyond communication, offering platforms for project management and teamwork. Tools like Trello, Asana, and Monday.com provide users with the ability to create tasks, assign responsibilities, and track progress in real-time. These platforms offer visual representations of projects, such as boards and timelines, making it easy to monitor deadlines and milestones. For beginners, utilizing collaboration tools can lead to more efficient project management and a clearer understanding of team dynamics.

Cloud storage solutions, such as Google Drive, Dropbox, and OneDrive, play a crucial role in collaboration by enabling users to store, share, and access files from anywhere with an internet connection. These tools offer features like version control, file sharing permissions, and real-time editing, ensuring that team members can work together seamlessly. For beginners, understanding how to effectively use cloud storage solutions can lead to more organized and accessible information sharing.

The integration of communication and collaboration tools with other software applications is a key feature that enhances their functionality. By connecting with tools like CRM systems, marketing automation platforms, and productivity apps, users can streamline workflows and ensure that information is consistent across all channels. This integration reduces the need for manual data entry and minimizes the risk of errors, allowing teams to focus on their core tasks. For beginners, understanding the importance of integration can lead to more efficient and effective use of communication and collaboration tools.

Security is a critical consideration when using communication and collaboration tools, as they often involve the exchange of sensitive information. It's essential to choose tools that offer robust security features, such as encryption, two-factor authentication, and regular security updates. These measures protect against unauthorized access and ensure that data is safeguarded. For beginners, understanding the importance of security in communication and collaboration tools is crucial to maintaining trust and compliance with data protection regulations.

Customization is another significant advantage of communication and collaboration tools, allowing users to tailor the platforms to their specific needs and workflows. Whether it's customizing notification settings, creating personalized dashboards, or setting up automated workflows, these tools offer flexibility to accommodate diverse requirements. For beginners, the ability to customize the software ensures that it aligns with their unique work processes and enhances overall productivity.

The learning curve associated with communication and collaboration tools can be a concern for beginners. However, many providers offer user-friendly interfaces and provide resources such as tutorials, webinars, and customer support to help users get started. By investing time in learning how to use these tools effectively, beginners can unlock significant benefits in terms of efficiency and collaboration.

Cost savings are a tangible benefit of communication and collaboration tools, as they reduce the need for physical meetings and minimize travel expenses. By enabling remote work and virtual collaboration, businesses can allocate resources more effectively and reduce operational costs. This financial advantage is particularly appealing to small businesses and startups looking to optimize their operations without incurring significant expenses.

Scalability is a critical consideration for businesses looking to implement communication and collaboration tools. As organizations grow and evolve, their communication and collaboration needs may change. Choosing tools that can scale with the organization ensures that they remain relevant and effective over time. For beginners, understanding the importance of scalability is key to selecting solutions that will support long-term growth and success.

Communication and collaboration tools offer a comprehensive suite of features designed to enhance interaction, streamline processes, and improve overall productivity. By understanding and leveraging these tools, beginners can take control of their communication and collaboration efforts, building stronger, more cohesive teams. As technology continues to evolve, the capabilities of these tools will only expand, offering even more opportunities for optimization and innovation.

AI and Machine Learning Applications

AI and machine learning have become integral components of modern technology, transforming industries and reshaping the way we interact with the world. These applications are not just confined to tech giants or research labs; they are increasingly accessible to businesses, educators, and individuals, offering a myriad of opportunities for innovation and efficiency. For beginners, understanding the practical applications of AI and machine learning can open doors to new possibilities and enhance their ability to leverage these technologies effectively.

One of the most prominent applications of AI is in the realm of data analysis. Machine learning algorithms excel at processing vast amounts of data, identifying patterns, and making predictions. This capability is invaluable for businesses seeking to gain insights from customer data, optimize operations, or forecast market trends. For beginners, familiarizing themselves with tools like Python and libraries such as TensorFlow or Scikit-learn can provide a solid foundation for exploring data-driven decision-making.

In the healthcare sector, AI and machine learning are revolutionizing diagnostics and treatment planning. Algorithms can analyze medical images, such as X-rays or MRIs, with remarkable accuracy, assisting doctors in identifying conditions that might be missed by the human eye. Additionally, machine learning models can predict patient outcomes based on historical data, enabling personalized treatment plans. For beginners interested in healthcare applications, understanding the ethical considerations and data privacy regulations is crucial to responsibly harnessing these technologies.

The financial industry has also embraced AI and machine learning, utilizing them for tasks ranging from fraud detection to algorithmic trading. Machine learning models can analyze transaction data in real-time, identifying anomalies that may indicate fraudulent activity. In trading, AI algorithms can process market data at lightning speed, executing trades based on complex strategies. Beginners looking to enter the financial sector should focus on developing skills in quantitative analysis and understanding the regulatory landscape to effectively apply AI solutions.

In the realm of customer service, AI-powered chatbots and virtual assistants are becoming increasingly common. These tools use natural language processing to understand and respond to customer inquiries, providing instant support and freeing up human agents for more complex tasks. For businesses, implementing AI-driven customer service solutions can lead to improved customer satisfaction and reduced operational costs. Beginners can start by exploring platforms like Dialogflow or Microsoft Bot Framework to create their own conversational agents.

AI and machine learning are also making significant strides in the field of autonomous vehicles. Self-driving cars rely on a combination of sensors, cameras, and machine learning algorithms to navigate roads and make real-time decisions. These technologies have the potential to reduce accidents, improve traffic flow, and provide mobility solutions for those unable to drive. For beginners interested in autonomous systems, gaining knowledge in robotics, computer vision, and sensor technologies is essential to contributing to this rapidly evolving field.

In agriculture, AI applications are enhancing productivity and sustainability. Machine learning models can analyze satellite imagery to monitor crop health, predict yields, and optimize irrigation. Drones equipped with AI technology can survey fields, identifying areas that require attention. These innovations enable farmers to make data-driven decisions, reducing waste and improving efficiency. Beginners can explore platforms like Google Earth Engine or open-source tools like QGIS to start working with geospatial data in agriculture.

The entertainment industry is also leveraging AI and machine learning to create personalized experiences. Streaming services use recommendation algorithms to suggest content based on user preferences, while AI-driven tools assist in content creation, such as generating music or editing videos. For beginners interested in the creative applications of AI, exploring tools like Adobe Sensei or experimenting with generative adversarial networks (GANs) can provide a glimpse into the future of entertainment.

In education, AI and machine learning are transforming the way we learn and teach. Adaptive learning platforms use machine learning algorithms to tailor educational content to individual students, addressing their unique strengths and weaknesses. AI-driven analytics can provide educators with insights into student performance, enabling targeted interventions. For beginners in the education sector, understanding how to integrate AI tools into curricula and ensuring equitable access to technology are key considerations.

AI and machine learning are also playing a crucial role in addressing environmental challenges. Predictive models can forecast weather patterns, helping communities prepare for natural disasters. AI algorithms can optimize energy consumption in smart grids, reducing carbon footprints. For beginners passionate about environmental sustainability, exploring AI applications in climate science and renewable energy can lead to impactful contributions.

The ethical implications of AI and machine learning cannot be overlooked. As these technologies become more pervasive, concerns about bias, privacy, and accountability arise. It is essential for beginners to understand the ethical frameworks and guidelines that govern AI development and deployment. Engaging with interdisciplinary perspectives and staying informed about policy developments can help ensure that AI applications are used responsibly and for the greater good.

AI and machine learning applications are vast and varied, offering opportunities for innovation across numerous sectors. By understanding the practical uses of these technologies and developing the necessary skills, beginners can position themselves at the forefront of this technological revolution. As AI continues to evolve, the potential for new applications and advancements will only grow, paving the way for a future where AI is an integral part of everyday life.

Chapter 3: Implementing Automation in Your Workflow

Assessing Your Current Workflow

Understanding your current workflow is a crucial step in optimizing productivity and efficiency. It involves a thorough examination of how tasks are performed, identifying bottlenecks, and recognizing areas for improvement. This process is not just about scrutinizing the steps you take but also about understanding the tools and resources you use, the time spent on each task, and the outcomes achieved. By assessing your workflow, you can make informed decisions that lead to enhanced performance and satisfaction.

Begin by mapping out your existing workflow. This involves documenting each step of your process from start to finish. Whether you're managing a project, handling daily tasks, or overseeing a team, having a visual representation of your workflow can provide clarity. Use flowcharts or diagrams to illustrate the sequence of actions, decision points, and dependencies. This visual aid helps in identifying redundant steps or areas where tasks can be streamlined.

Once your workflow is mapped, analyze the time spent on each task. Time tracking tools can be invaluable in this regard, offering insights into how long each activity takes and highlighting inefficiencies. Are there tasks that consistently take longer than expected? Are there periods of downtime that could be better utilized? Understanding time allocation allows you to prioritize tasks effectively and allocate resources where they are most needed.

Consider the tools and technology you currently use. Are they facilitating your workflow, or are they hindering it? Sometimes, outdated or incompatible tools can create unnecessary friction, slowing down processes and causing frustration. Evaluate whether there are more efficient alternatives available. For instance, project management software can streamline communication and task tracking, while automation tools can handle repetitive tasks, freeing up time for more strategic activities.

Communication is another critical aspect of workflow assessment. Examine how information is shared within your team or organization. Are there clear channels for communication, or do messages get lost in a sea of emails and messages? Effective communication tools and protocols can significantly enhance collaboration and ensure that everyone is on the same page. Consider implementing regular check-ins or using collaborative platforms to keep everyone informed and engaged.

Feedback from team members or colleagues can provide valuable insights into your workflow. Encourage open discussions about what works well and what doesn't. Often, those involved in the day-to-day operations can offer perspectives that might not be immediately apparent. This collaborative approach not only fosters a sense of ownership but also uncovers potential improvements that might have been overlooked.

Identify bottlenecks or pain points in your workflow. These are areas where tasks get delayed or where resources are stretched thin. Bottlenecks can occur due to various reasons, such as a lack of resources, inefficient processes, or unclear responsibilities. Once identified, work on strategies to alleviate these bottlenecks. This might involve redistributing tasks, investing in additional resources, or redefining roles and responsibilities.

Flexibility is key when assessing your workflow. Be open to change and willing to adapt. The business landscape is constantly evolving, and what worked yesterday might not be effective today. Regularly revisiting and updating your workflow ensures that it remains relevant and efficient. This proactive approach allows you to stay ahead of potential challenges and seize new opportunities as they arise.

Consider the outcomes of your current workflow. Are you meeting your goals and objectives? Are there areas where performance could be improved? Assessing outcomes provides a benchmark for success and highlights areas for growth. Set clear, measurable goals and track progress regularly. This not only keeps you focused but also provides motivation and a sense of accomplishment as milestones are achieved.

Incorporate feedback loops into your workflow. These are mechanisms for continuous improvement, allowing you to refine processes based on real-world results. Feedback loops can be formal, such as regular performance reviews, or informal, such as casual check-ins with team members. The key is to create a culture of continuous learning and improvement, where feedback is valued and acted upon.

Finally, consider the human element of your workflow. Are team members engaged and motivated? Are they empowered to make decisions and contribute ideas? A positive work environment fosters creativity and innovation, leading to improved performance and satisfaction. Encourage a culture of collaboration and support, where team members feel valued and appreciated.

Assessing your current workflow is an ongoing process that requires attention and commitment. By taking the time to understand and optimize your workflow, you can enhance productivity, improve outcomes, and create a more fulfilling work experience. This proactive approach not only benefits you but also contributes to the overall success of your team or organization.

Identifying Areas for Improvement

Recognizing areas for improvement is a vital step in personal and professional growth. It involves a keen understanding of one's strengths and weaknesses, as well as the ability to critically evaluate processes, behaviors, and outcomes. This self-awareness and analytical mindset can lead to significant enhancements in efficiency, productivity, and satisfaction. By identifying areas for improvement, individuals and organizations can implement targeted strategies that foster development and success.

Begin by conducting a thorough self-assessment or organizational review. This involves taking a step back and objectively evaluating current practices, habits, and results. Consider what is working well and what is not. Are there recurring challenges or obstacles that hinder progress? Are there patterns of behavior that lead to suboptimal outcomes?

This introspective approach requires honesty and openness, as it may reveal uncomfortable truths that need to be addressed.

Feedback from others can provide valuable insights into areas for improvement. Seek input from colleagues, mentors, or peers who can offer different perspectives. They may notice things that you have overlooked or provide constructive criticism that can guide your development. Encourage open and honest communication, and be receptive to feedback, even if it is difficult to hear. This collaborative approach not only fosters a culture of continuous improvement but also strengthens relationships and builds trust.

Analyze the outcomes of your efforts. Are you achieving the desired results? Are there areas where performance could be enhanced? Setting clear, measurable goals and tracking progress can provide a benchmark for success. If goals are consistently unmet, it may indicate a need for change. Consider whether the goals themselves are realistic and achievable, or if the strategies employed to reach them need adjustment. This outcome-based analysis allows for targeted improvements that align with overarching objectives.

Consider the resources available to you. Are there tools, technologies, or support systems that could enhance your performance? Sometimes, a lack of resources can create unnecessary challenges and hinder progress. Evaluate whether there are more efficient alternatives or additional resources that could be leveraged. Investing in the right tools and support can lead to significant improvements in efficiency and effectiveness.

Examine your time management practices. Are you using your time effectively, or are there areas where it could be better allocated? Time is a finite resource, and how it is managed can have a profound impact on productivity and success. Consider whether there are tasks that could be delegated, automated, or eliminated altogether. Prioritizing tasks and setting clear deadlines can help ensure that time is spent on activities that align with goals and objectives.

Reflect on your skills and competencies. Are there areas where you could benefit from additional training or development? Continuous learning and skill enhancement are essential for staying competitive and relevant in today's fast-paced world. Identify opportunities for growth, whether through formal education, workshops, or self-directed learning. Investing in your development not only enhances your capabilities but also boosts confidence and motivation.

Consider the impact of your actions on others. Are there ways to improve collaboration, communication, or teamwork? Building strong relationships and fostering a positive work environment can lead to improved outcomes and satisfaction. Encourage open dialogue, active listening, and mutual respect. Recognize and celebrate the contributions of others, and work together to identify areas for improvement that benefit the entire team or organization.

Embrace a mindset of continuous improvement. This involves being open to change and willing to adapt. The world is constantly evolving, and what worked yesterday may not be effective today. Regularly revisiting and updating practices, processes, and goals ensures that they remain relevant and effective. This proactive approach allows you to stay ahead of potential challenges and seize new opportunities as they arise.

Identify potential barriers to improvement. Are there external factors or internal resistance that may hinder progress? Understanding these barriers allows for the development of strategies to overcome them. This may involve addressing fears or misconceptions, building consensus, or creating a supportive environment that encourages change. By proactively addressing barriers, you can create a smoother path to improvement.

Finally, recognize that improvement is an ongoing journey, not a destination. It requires commitment, perseverance, and a willingness to learn from both successes and failures. Celebrate progress and achievements, but also remain vigilant for new opportunities for growth. By maintaining a focus on continuous improvement, you can achieve lasting success and fulfillment in both personal and professional endeavors.

Choosing the Right Tools

Selecting the appropriate tools is a crucial step in any endeavor, whether it be a personal project or a professional undertaking. The right tools can enhance efficiency, improve outcomes, and make the process more enjoyable. Conversely, the wrong tools can lead to frustration, wasted time, and subpar results. Understanding how to choose the right tools involves assessing your needs, evaluating available options, and making informed decisions that align with your goals.

Begin by clearly defining the objectives of your project or task. What are you trying to achieve, and what are the specific requirements? Understanding the scope and nature of your work will guide you in identifying the tools that are best suited to your needs. Consider the complexity of the task, the desired outcomes, and any constraints you may face, such as budget or time limitations. This foundational step ensures that you have a clear vision of what you need to accomplish, which will inform your tool selection process.

Once you have a clear understanding of your objectives, conduct thorough research on the available tools. This involves exploring different options, comparing features, and evaluating their suitability for your specific needs. Look for tools that offer the functionality you require, as well as any additional features that may enhance your work. Consider the reputation and reliability of the tools, as well as user reviews and testimonials. This research phase is critical in ensuring that you make an informed decision based on comprehensive information.

Consider the ease of use and learning curve associated with each tool. Some tools may offer advanced features but require significant time and effort to master. Others may be more intuitive and user-friendly, allowing you to get started quickly. Evaluate your own skills and experience, as well as the time you are willing to invest in learning a new tool. Choosing a tool that aligns with your skill level and learning preferences can make the process more enjoyable and efficient.

Evaluate the compatibility of the tools with your existing systems and processes. Will the tool integrate seamlessly with other tools or software you are already using? Compatibility is an important consideration, as it can impact the efficiency and effectiveness of your work. Look for tools that offer integration options or are designed to work well with other commonly used tools. This ensures that you can maintain a smooth workflow and avoid potential disruptions.

Consider the cost of the tools and your budget constraints. While some tools may offer advanced features, they may also come with a higher price tag. Evaluate whether the benefits of the tool justify the cost, and consider any ongoing expenses, such as subscription fees or maintenance costs. Look for cost-effective alternatives that offer the functionality you need without exceeding your budget. Remember that the most expensive tool is not always the best choice; it's about finding the right balance between cost and value.

Seek recommendations and advice from others who have experience with the tools you are considering. Colleagues, mentors, or online communities can provide valuable insights and firsthand experiences that can guide your decision-making process. They may offer tips on how to get the most out of a tool or highlight potential drawbacks that you may not have considered. This collaborative approach can provide a broader perspective and help you make a more informed choice.

Test the tools before making a final decision. Many tools offer free trials or demo versions that allow you to explore their features and functionality. Take advantage of these opportunities to get hands-on experience and assess whether the tool meets your needs. Pay attention to how the tool performs, its ease of use, and whether it enhances your workflow. This practical evaluation can provide valuable insights and help you make a confident decision.

Reflect on the long-term implications of your tool choice. Will the tool continue to meet your needs as your project or organization evolves? Consider whether the tool offers scalability and flexibility to accommodate future growth or changes. This forward-thinking approach ensures that you choose a tool that will remain relevant and valuable over time, reducing the need for frequent changes or upgrades.

Finally, trust your instincts and make a decision that feels right for you. While research and recommendations are important, ultimately, you are the one who will be using the tool. Consider how the tool aligns with your personal preferences, work style, and goals. A tool that feels comfortable and intuitive to you is more likely to enhance your productivity and satisfaction.

Choosing the right tools is a thoughtful and deliberate process that requires careful consideration and evaluation. By taking the time to assess your needs, research options, and test tools, you can make informed decisions that support your success. The right tools can empower you to achieve your goals with greater efficiency and effectiveness, making the journey more rewarding and enjoyable.

Integration Strategies

Integrating new strategies into existing frameworks can be a daunting task, yet it is essential for growth and adaptation in any field. The process of integration involves blending new ideas, tools, or processes with established systems to create a cohesive and efficient operation. This requires careful planning, a clear understanding of objectives, and a willingness to adapt and evolve. By approaching integration strategically, you can ensure a smooth transition and maximize the benefits of new strategies.

Begin by assessing the current state of your systems and processes. Understanding the strengths and weaknesses of your existing framework is crucial in identifying areas where integration can bring the most value. Conduct a thorough analysis of your operations, focusing on efficiency, effectiveness, and any gaps or challenges that need to be addressed. This assessment provides a baseline from which you can measure the impact of new strategies and identify opportunities for improvement.

Once you have a clear understanding of your current systems, define the objectives of the integration. What are you hoping to achieve by incorporating new strategies? Whether it's improving efficiency, enhancing performance, or expanding capabilities, having clear goals will guide your integration efforts and help you measure success. Consider both short-term and long-term objectives, and ensure that they align with your overall vision and mission.

With your objectives in mind, develop a detailed integration plan. This plan should outline the steps required to incorporate new strategies into your existing framework, including timelines, resources, and responsibilities. Consider potential challenges and risks, and develop contingency plans to address them. A well-structured plan provides a roadmap for the integration process and ensures that all stakeholders are aligned and informed.

Communication is a critical component of successful integration. Ensure that all stakeholders are aware of the integration plan, objectives, and their roles in the process. Open and transparent communication fosters collaboration and buy-in, reducing resistance and facilitating a smoother transition.

Regular updates and feedback loops allow for adjustments and improvements, ensuring that the integration remains on track and aligned with objectives.

Training and support are essential in helping individuals adapt to new strategies. Provide comprehensive training programs that equip team members with the skills and knowledge they need to effectively implement and utilize new strategies. Offer ongoing support and resources to address any challenges or questions that may arise. By investing in training and support, you empower individuals to embrace change and contribute to the success of the integration.

Monitor and evaluate the integration process to ensure that it is achieving the desired outcomes. Establish key performance indicators (KPIs) that align with your objectives and track progress regularly. Analyze data and feedback to identify areas for improvement and make necessary adjustments. Continuous monitoring and evaluation allow you to optimize the integration process and maximize the benefits of new strategies.

Flexibility and adaptability are crucial in navigating the complexities of integration. Be open to feedback and willing to make changes as needed. The integration process may reveal unexpected challenges or opportunities, and being adaptable allows you to respond effectively. Encourage a culture of innovation and continuous improvement, where individuals feel empowered to contribute ideas and solutions.

Celebrate successes and milestones throughout the integration process. Recognizing achievements boosts morale and reinforces the value of the new strategies. It also provides an opportunity to reflect on lessons learned and share best practices. Celebrating successes fosters a positive and motivated environment, encouraging continued commitment to the integration process.

Reflect on the long-term impact of the integration. Consider how the new strategies have enhanced your operations and contributed to your overall goals. Evaluate whether the integration has positioned you for future growth and success. This reflection provides valuable insights and informs future integration efforts, ensuring that you continue to evolve and adapt in a dynamic environment.

Integration strategies require careful planning, effective communication, and a commitment to continuous improvement. By approaching integration strategically, you can successfully blend new strategies with existing systems, enhancing efficiency and effectiveness. The process of integration is an opportunity for growth and innovation, empowering you to achieve your goals and drive success.

Setting Up Automation Processes

Automation processes have become an integral part of modern operations, offering a way to streamline tasks, reduce human error, and increase efficiency. Setting up these processes requires a thoughtful approach, ensuring that they align with your objectives and integrate seamlessly into your existing systems. By carefully planning and executing automation strategies, you can unlock significant benefits and drive your operations forward.

The first step in setting up automation processes is identifying the tasks or workflows that would benefit most from automation. Look for repetitive, time-consuming tasks that require minimal human intervention. These are prime candidates for automation, as they can free up valuable time and resources for more strategic activities. Consider tasks such as data entry, report generation, and routine communications, which often consume significant time and effort.

Once you've identified potential tasks for automation, evaluate the tools and technologies available to support your efforts. There is a wide range of automation software and platforms, each with its own strengths and capabilities. Research and compare options to find the best fit for your needs, considering factors such as ease of use, scalability, and integration with existing systems. It's essential to choose tools that align with your objectives and can grow with your organization.

With the right tools in place, map out the processes you wish to automate. This involves breaking down each task into its component steps and identifying the inputs, outputs, and decision points involved. A clear understanding of the process flow is crucial for successful automation, as it allows you to design workflows that accurately replicate the task. Documenting these processes also provides a valuable reference for future optimization and troubleshooting.

Designing the automation workflow is a critical step in the setup process. Use the insights gained from mapping out the process to create a detailed workflow that outlines each step and decision point. Consider potential exceptions or variations in the process and incorporate logic to handle these scenarios. A well-designed workflow ensures that the automation process runs smoothly and delivers consistent results.

Testing is an essential part of setting up automation processes. Before deploying the automation in a live environment, conduct thorough testing to ensure that it functions as intended. Test the workflow with various inputs and scenarios to identify any issues or areas for improvement. This testing phase allows you to refine the process and address any potential problems before they impact operations.

Once testing is complete, deploy the automation process and monitor its performance. Keep a close eye on key metrics and performance indicators to ensure that the automation is delivering the desired results. Regular monitoring allows you to identify any issues or inefficiencies and make necessary adjustments. It also provides valuable insights into the impact of automation on your operations, helping you measure success and identify opportunities for further optimization.

Training and support are crucial components of successful automation implementation. Ensure that team members understand the automation processes and their role in managing and maintaining them. Provide training and resources to help individuals adapt to the new workflows and address any questions or challenges that may arise. Ongoing support ensures that the automation processes continue to operate smoothly and deliver value.

As you gain experience with automation, look for opportunities to expand and optimize your processes. Consider additional tasks or workflows that could benefit from automation and explore ways to enhance existing processes. Continuous improvement is key to maximizing the benefits of automation, allowing you to adapt to changing needs and drive ongoing efficiency gains.

Reflect on the impact of automation on your operations and objectives. Consider how the processes have improved efficiency, reduced errors, and freed up resources for more strategic activities. Evaluate whether the automation has positioned you for future growth and success, and use these insights to inform future automation efforts. By continually assessing and optimizing your automation processes, you can ensure that they remain a valuable asset to your organization.

Setting up automation processes requires careful planning, execution, and ongoing optimization. By identifying the right tasks, selecting appropriate tools, and designing effective workflows, you can successfully integrate automation into your operations. The benefits of automation are significant, offering increased efficiency, reduced errors, and the ability to focus on more strategic activities. With a thoughtful approach and commitment to continuous improvement, you can harness the power of automation to drive success and achieve your goals.

Scheduling and Calendar Management

Effective scheduling and calendar management are essential skills for anyone looking to optimize their time and increase productivity. In a world where demands on our time are ever-increasing, mastering these skills can make the difference between feeling overwhelmed and maintaining control over your day. By implementing strategic scheduling techniques and utilizing calendar tools effectively, you can ensure that your time is spent on activities that align with your goals and priorities.

The foundation of successful scheduling begins with understanding your priorities. Before diving into the mechanics of calendar management, take a step back to evaluate what truly matters to you. Consider both personal and professional goals, and identify the tasks and activities that will help you achieve them. This clarity will serve as a guiding light when making decisions about how to allocate your time.

Once you have a clear understanding of your priorities, it's time to translate them into actionable plans. Start by breaking down your goals into smaller, manageable tasks. This not only makes them less daunting but also provides a clear roadmap for what needs to be accomplished. Assign deadlines to each task, ensuring that they are realistic and achievable. This process of task decomposition and deadline setting is crucial for effective scheduling.

With your tasks and deadlines in place, it's time to leverage your calendar as a powerful tool for time management. Choose a calendar system that suits your needs, whether it's a digital platform or a traditional paper planner. The key is to find a system that you are comfortable with and that integrates seamlessly into your daily routine. Consistency is vital, so commit to using your chosen calendar system regularly.

Begin by blocking out time for your most important tasks and activities. These are the non-negotiables that align with your priorities and contribute directly to your goals. Schedule these blocks during your peak productivity hours, when you are most focused and energized. By dedicating specific time slots to these tasks, you ensure that they receive the attention they deserve and reduce the risk of them being overshadowed by less important activities.

In addition to scheduling time for important tasks, it's essential to allocate time for routine activities and responsibilities. These may include meetings, administrative tasks, and personal commitments. While they may not directly contribute to your goals, they are necessary components of your daily life. By scheduling them in advance, you can manage your time more effectively and prevent them from encroaching on your priority tasks.

One of the most powerful techniques in calendar management is time blocking. This involves dividing your day into blocks of time dedicated to specific activities or types of work. For example, you might allocate a block of time in the morning for focused work, followed by a block for meetings, and another for administrative tasks. Time blocking helps you maintain focus and reduces the mental load of constantly switching between different types of work.

While scheduling is about planning, it's also important to remain flexible and adaptable. Life is unpredictable, and unexpected events or changes in priorities can disrupt even the most well-laid plans. Build buffer time into your schedule to accommodate unforeseen circumstances and allow for adjustments. This flexibility ensures that you can respond to changes without feeling overwhelmed or derailed.

Regularly reviewing and adjusting your schedule is a crucial aspect of effective calendar management. Set aside time each week to reflect on your progress, evaluate how well your schedule aligns with your priorities, and make any necessary adjustments. This practice of regular review helps you stay on track and ensures that your time is being spent in alignment with your goals.

Incorporating breaks and downtime into your schedule is equally important. While it may seem counterintuitive, taking regular breaks can actually enhance productivity and prevent burnout. Schedule short breaks throughout your day to recharge and refocus. Additionally, ensure that you allocate time for leisure activities and self-care, as these are essential for maintaining overall well-being and sustaining long-term productivity.

Communication plays a vital role in scheduling and calendar management, especially in a collaborative environment. Share your schedule with colleagues, family members, or anyone else who may be impacted by your availability. This transparency fosters understanding and cooperation, reducing the likelihood of scheduling conflicts and ensuring that everyone is on the same page.

Technology can be a valuable ally in calendar management, offering tools and features that enhance efficiency and organization. Explore calendar apps and software that offer features such as reminders, notifications, and integration with other productivity tools. These features can help you stay on top of your schedule and ensure that nothing falls through the cracks.

Ultimately, effective scheduling and calendar management are about making intentional choices about how you spend your time. By aligning your schedule with your priorities, leveraging time-blocking techniques, and remaining flexible, you can take control of your time and achieve your goals with greater ease. The journey to mastering these skills is ongoing, but with practice and commitment, you can transform your approach to time management and unlock your full potential.

Automated Data Entry

Automated data entry has revolutionized the way businesses handle information, offering a seamless and efficient alternative to manual data processing. In an era where data is the backbone of decision-making, the ability to automate data entry processes can significantly enhance productivity, accuracy, and overall operational efficiency. For beginners venturing into this domain, understanding the fundamentals of automated data entry and its practical applications is crucial.

At its core, automated data entry involves the use of technology to capture, process, and store data without human intervention. This can be achieved through various tools and software designed to streamline the data entry process. Optical Character Recognition (OCR) technology, for instance, is widely used to convert different types of documents, such as scanned paper documents, PDFs, or images captured by a digital camera, into editable and searchable data. By recognizing text within these documents, OCR eliminates the need for manual data entry, reducing the risk of errors and saving valuable time.

Another powerful tool in the realm of automated data entry is Robotic Process Automation (RPA). RPA involves the use of software robots or "bots" to perform repetitive tasks that were traditionally carried out by humans. These bots can be programmed to mimic human interactions with digital systems, such as logging into applications, entering data, and performing calculations. By automating these routine tasks, RPA frees up human resources to focus on more strategic and value-added activities.

The implementation of automated data entry systems begins with identifying the specific data entry tasks that can be automated. This requires a thorough analysis of existing processes to pinpoint areas where automation can bring the most significant benefits. Consider tasks that are repetitive, time-consuming, and prone to human error. These are prime candidates for automation and can yield substantial improvements in efficiency and accuracy.

Once the tasks have been identified, the next step is to select the appropriate tools and software for automation. This decision should be guided by factors such as the complexity of the tasks, the volume of data to be processed, and the level of integration required with existing systems. It's essential to choose solutions that are scalable and adaptable to future needs, ensuring that the automation strategy remains effective as the business grows and evolves.

Training and support are critical components of a successful automated data entry implementation. Employees need to be equipped with the knowledge and skills to operate and manage the new systems effectively. This may involve training sessions, workshops, or online courses to familiarize them with the tools and processes involved. Additionally, ongoing support should be provided to address any technical issues or challenges that may arise, ensuring a smooth transition to automated data entry.

Data security is a paramount consideration when implementing automated data entry systems. With the increasing reliance on digital data, safeguarding sensitive information from unauthorized access and breaches is crucial. Implement robust security measures, such as encryption, access controls, and regular audits, to protect data integrity and confidentiality. Compliance with relevant data protection regulations, such as the General Data Protection Regulation (GDPR), should also be a priority to avoid legal repercussions.

The benefits of automated data entry extend beyond efficiency and accuracy. By reducing the reliance on manual data entry, businesses can achieve significant cost savings. The reduction in labor costs, coupled with the minimization of errors and associated rework, can lead to substantial financial gains. Moreover, automation enables faster data processing, allowing businesses to make timely and informed decisions based on real-time data insights.

Despite its advantages, automated data entry is not without its challenges. One common hurdle is the initial investment required for implementing automation solutions. While the long-term benefits often outweigh the costs, the upfront expenditure can be a barrier for some businesses. It's essential to conduct a cost-benefit analysis to assess the potential return on investment and make informed decisions about automation initiatives.

Another challenge is the potential resistance to change from employees accustomed to traditional data entry methods. Change management strategies, such as clear communication, employee involvement, and incentives, can help overcome this resistance and foster a culture of innovation and continuous improvement.

As technology continues to advance, the capabilities of automated data entry systems are expected to expand further. Emerging technologies, such as artificial intelligence and machine learning, hold the promise of even greater automation potential, enabling systems to learn and adapt to new data patterns and processes. Staying abreast of these developments and continuously exploring opportunities for innovation will be key to maintaining a competitive edge in the ever-evolving landscape of data management.

In conclusion, automated data entry offers a transformative approach to handling data, providing businesses with the tools to enhance efficiency, accuracy, and decision-making capabilities. By understanding the fundamentals of automation, selecting the right tools, and addressing potential challenges, beginners can successfully navigate the transition to automated data entry and unlock its full potential. The journey may require investment and adaptation, but the rewards in terms of productivity and operational excellence are well worth the effort.

Invoicing and Billing Automation

Invoicing and billing automation has emerged as a game-changer for businesses seeking to streamline their financial operations. The traditional methods of handling invoices and bills, often characterized by manual data entry and paper-based processes, are not only time-consuming but also prone to errors. Automation offers a solution that enhances efficiency, accuracy, and overall financial management.

At the heart of invoicing and billing automation is the use of software solutions designed to handle the entire process with minimal human intervention. These systems can generate invoices, send them to clients, track payments, and even send reminders for overdue payments. By automating these tasks, businesses can significantly reduce the administrative burden on their staff, allowing them to focus on more strategic activities.

One of the primary benefits of invoicing and billing automation is the reduction in errors. Manual data entry is susceptible to mistakes, which can lead to discrepancies in financial records and potential disputes with clients. Automated systems, on the other hand, ensure that data is accurately captured and processed, minimizing the risk of errors. This not only improves the accuracy of financial records but also enhances the credibility of the business in the eyes of its clients.

Time savings is another significant advantage of automation. The process of creating, sending, and tracking invoices manually can be labor-intensive and time-consuming. Automated systems can perform these tasks in a fraction of the time, freeing up valuable resources for other important functions. This increased efficiency can lead to faster payment cycles, improving cash flow and financial stability.

For businesses dealing with a large volume of transactions, scalability is a crucial consideration. Automated invoicing and billing systems are designed to handle high volumes of data, making them ideal for growing businesses. As the business expands, the system can easily accommodate the increased workload without compromising on performance or accuracy. This scalability ensures that the invoicing and billing process remains efficient and effective, regardless of the size of the business.

Customization is another key feature of automated invoicing and billing systems. Businesses can tailor the system to meet their specific needs, whether it's customizing invoice templates, setting up recurring billing for subscription services, or integrating with existing accounting software. This flexibility allows businesses to create a seamless and personalized invoicing experience for their clients, enhancing customer satisfaction and loyalty.

Security is a paramount concern when it comes to financial transactions. Automated invoicing and billing systems are equipped with robust security measures to protect sensitive financial data. Encryption, secure access controls, and regular security audits are some of the features that ensure data integrity and confidentiality. By safeguarding financial information, businesses can build trust with their clients and avoid potential legal issues related to data breaches.

The implementation of invoicing and billing automation begins with selecting the right software solution. Businesses should consider factors such as ease of use, integration capabilities, and cost when choosing a system. It's important to select a solution that aligns with the business's specific needs and goals, ensuring a smooth transition to automation.

Training and support are essential components of a successful implementation. Employees need to be familiar with the new system and understand how to use it effectively. This may involve training sessions, workshops, or online resources to equip staff with the necessary skills. Ongoing support should also be available to address any technical issues or challenges that may arise, ensuring that the system operates smoothly and efficiently.

Despite its many benefits, invoicing and billing automation is not without its challenges. One common hurdle is the initial investment required for implementing the system. While the long-term benefits often outweigh the costs, the upfront expenditure can be a barrier for some businesses. Conducting a cost-benefit analysis can help businesses assess the potential return on investment and make informed decisions about automation initiatives.

Another challenge is the potential resistance to change from employees accustomed to traditional invoicing methods. Change management strategies, such as clear communication, employee involvement, and incentives, can help overcome this resistance and foster a culture of innovation and continuous improvement.

As technology continues to evolve, the capabilities of invoicing and billing automation systems are expected to expand further. Emerging technologies hold the promise of even greater automation potential, enabling systems to learn and adapt to new data patterns and processes. Staying abreast of these developments and continuously exploring opportunities for innovation will be key to maintaining a competitive edge in the ever-evolving landscape of financial management.

Invoicing and billing automation offers a transformative approach to financial operations, providing businesses with the tools to enhance efficiency, accuracy, and decision-making capabilities. By understanding the fundamentals of automation, selecting the right tools, and addressing potential challenges, businesses can successfully navigate the transition to automated invoicing and billing and unlock its full potential. The journey may require investment and adaptation, but the rewards in terms of productivity and operational excellence are well worth the effort.

Travel and Expense Management

Travel and expense management is a crucial aspect of business operations, particularly for companies with employees who frequently travel for work. Managing these expenses efficiently can lead to significant cost savings and improved financial oversight. The process involves tracking, reporting, and reimbursing travel-related expenses, ensuring compliance with company policies, and optimizing travel budgets.

One of the first steps in effective travel and expense management is establishing clear policies. These policies should outline what constitutes a reimbursable expense, the process for submitting expense reports, and any limits or restrictions on spending. By setting clear guidelines, businesses can prevent misunderstandings and ensure that employees are aware of their responsibilities when it comes to managing travel expenses.

Technology plays a pivotal role in streamlining travel and expense management. Expense management software can automate many aspects of the process, from capturing receipts to generating reports. These tools often integrate with other financial systems, providing a seamless flow of data and reducing the need for manual data entry. By leveraging technology, businesses can enhance accuracy, reduce processing times, and gain better visibility into their travel expenses.

Mobile applications have become increasingly popular in the realm of travel and expense management. These apps allow employees to capture receipts and submit expense reports on the go, eliminating the need to keep track of paper receipts. This not only simplifies the process for employees but also ensures that expenses are reported in a timely manner. Real-time reporting can help businesses monitor spending patterns and identify any potential issues before they escalate.

Another important aspect of travel and expense management is compliance. Companies must ensure that their travel policies align with legal and regulatory requirements, such as tax laws and industry standards. Non-compliance can result in financial penalties and damage to the company's reputation. Regular audits and reviews of travel expenses can help identify any discrepancies and ensure adherence to policies.

Cost control is a key objective in travel and expense management. Businesses can achieve this by negotiating corporate rates with airlines, hotels, and car rental companies. Establishing partnerships with travel service providers can lead to discounted rates and added benefits, such as priority booking or upgrades. Additionally, implementing a pre-approval process for travel expenses can help control costs by ensuring that all travel plans align with the company's budget and objectives.

Employee training and communication are essential components of a successful travel and expense management strategy. Employees should be educated on the company's travel policies and the tools available to them for managing expenses. Regular communication can help reinforce these policies and address any questions or concerns employees may have. By fostering a culture of transparency and accountability, businesses can encourage responsible spending and compliance with travel policies.

Data analysis is a powerful tool for optimizing travel and expense management. By analyzing spending patterns and trends, businesses can identify areas for improvement and make informed decisions about their travel policies. For example, if data reveals that a significant portion of travel expenses is attributed to last-minute bookings, the company may consider implementing a policy that encourages early booking to take advantage of lower rates. Data-driven insights can lead to more strategic travel planning and cost savings.

Sustainability is an emerging consideration in travel and expense management. As businesses become more environmentally conscious, they are seeking ways to reduce their carbon footprint associated with business travel. This may involve encouraging the use of virtual meetings instead of in-person travel, selecting eco-friendly accommodations, or offsetting carbon emissions through sustainable initiatives. By incorporating sustainability into travel policies, businesses can demonstrate their commitment to environmental responsibility while potentially reducing costs.

The role of travel managers is evolving in response to changing business needs and technological advancements. Travel managers are now expected to be strategic partners who contribute to the company's overall goals. This involves collaborating with other departments, such as finance and human resources, to align travel policies with broader business objectives. Travel managers must also stay informed about industry trends and emerging technologies to continuously improve the travel and expense management process.

Challenges in travel and expense management can arise from various sources, such as fluctuating travel costs, currency exchange rates, and geopolitical events. Businesses must be prepared to adapt to these challenges by maintaining flexible travel policies and staying informed about global developments. Contingency planning can help mitigate the impact of unforeseen events on travel budgets and ensure business continuity.

Travel and expense management is a dynamic and multifaceted process that requires careful planning, effective communication, and the use of technology. By establishing clear policies, leveraging technology, and analyzing data, businesses can optimize their travel expenses and achieve greater financial control. As the business landscape continues to evolve, companies must remain agile and proactive in their approach to travel and expense management, ensuring that they are well-positioned to navigate the challenges and opportunities that lie ahead.

HR and Recruitment Automation

The landscape of human resources and recruitment has undergone a significant transformation with the advent of automation technologies. These advancements have revolutionized the way organizations attract, hire, and manage talent, offering a more efficient and streamlined approach to traditional HR processes. For businesses aiming to stay competitive in a rapidly evolving market, understanding and implementing HR and recruitment automation is no longer optional but essential.

Automation in HR begins with the recruitment process, where it can significantly reduce the time and effort involved in sourcing and screening candidates. Applicant tracking systems (ATS) are at the forefront of this transformation, enabling recruiters to manage large volumes of applications with ease. These systems automatically parse resumes, filter candidates based on predefined criteria, and rank them according to their suitability for the role. This not only accelerates the recruitment process but also ensures that only the most qualified candidates reach the interview stage.

Beyond initial screening, automation tools can enhance the candidate experience by providing timely and personalized communication. Chatbots, for instance, can engage with candidates throughout the application process, answering common queries and providing updates on their application status. This level of interaction helps maintain candidate interest and reduces the likelihood of losing top talent due to prolonged response times.

Interview scheduling is another area where automation proves invaluable. Coordinating interviews can be a logistical challenge, particularly when dealing with multiple candidates and interviewers. Automated scheduling tools eliminate the back-and-forth communication typically required to find mutually convenient times, allowing candidates to select interview slots based on their availability. This not only saves time for HR professionals but also demonstrates a commitment to efficiency and respect for the candidate's time.

Once candidates are selected, automation continues to play a crucial role in onboarding. Automated onboarding systems guide new hires through the necessary paperwork, training modules, and introductions to company culture. By providing a structured and consistent onboarding experience, these systems help new employees acclimate more quickly and effectively, leading to higher retention rates and increased productivity.

Performance management is another HR function that benefits from automation. Traditional performance reviews can be time-consuming and subjective, often leading to dissatisfaction among employees. Automated performance management systems offer a more objective and continuous approach, collecting data on employee performance throughout the year and providing real-time feedback. This allows managers to identify areas for improvement and recognize achievements promptly, fostering a culture of continuous development and engagement.

In addition to improving efficiency, HR automation can enhance decision-making through data analytics. By collecting and analyzing data on recruitment, employee performance, and turnover, organizations can gain valuable insights into their workforce. These insights can inform strategic decisions, such as identifying skill gaps, optimizing workforce planning, and tailoring employee development programs to meet future needs.

However, the implementation of HR and recruitment automation is not without its challenges. One of the primary concerns is the potential loss of the human touch in HR processes. While automation can handle repetitive and administrative tasks, it is essential to strike a balance between technology and human interaction. HR professionals must ensure that automation enhances rather than replaces personal engagement, particularly in areas such as employee relations and conflict resolution.

Data privacy and security are also critical considerations when implementing automation in HR. Organizations must ensure that the systems they use comply with data protection regulations and that sensitive employee information is safeguarded against unauthorized access. This requires robust security measures and regular audits to identify and address potential vulnerabilities.

To successfully integrate automation into HR and recruitment processes, organizations should adopt a strategic approach. This involves assessing current HR practices, identifying areas where automation can add value, and selecting the right tools to meet their specific needs. It is also important to involve HR professionals in the decision-making process, as their expertise and insights are invaluable in ensuring that automation aligns with organizational goals and culture.

Training and support are essential components of a successful automation strategy. HR professionals must be equipped with the skills and knowledge to effectively use automation tools and interpret the data they generate. Ongoing training and support can help ensure that HR teams remain agile and responsive to changing business needs and technological advancements.

The future of HR and recruitment lies in the seamless integration of automation technologies with human expertise. By embracing automation, organizations can enhance efficiency, improve the candidate and employee experience, and make more informed decisions. However, it is crucial to maintain a focus on the human element, ensuring that technology serves as an enabler rather than a replacement for meaningful human interaction. As businesses continue to navigate the complexities of the modern workforce, HR and recruitment automation will play an increasingly vital role in driving success and innovation.

Chapter 5: Enhancing Communication and Collaboration

Automated Email Responses

Crafting automated email responses is an art that balances efficiency with personalization. In a world where communication is instantaneous, businesses and individuals alike are inundated with emails. The challenge lies in managing this influx without sacrificing the quality of interaction. Automated email responses offer a solution, providing timely replies while freeing up valuable time for more complex tasks. However, the key to successful automation lies in creating responses that feel personal and relevant, rather than robotic and generic.

The first step in developing effective automated email responses is understanding the common types of inquiries or messages you receive. By categorizing these emails, you can tailor your automated responses to address specific needs. For instance, a business might receive frequent inquiries about product availability, shipping times, or return policies. By identifying these patterns, you can create targeted responses that provide the necessary information quickly and efficiently.

Once you've identified the types of emails you receive, it's important to craft responses that are clear, concise, and informative. An automated response should address the sender's query directly, providing the information they need without unnecessary fluff. This requires a deep understanding of your audience and their expectations. Consider the tone and language that will resonate with them, whether it's formal and professional or casual and friendly.

Personalization is a crucial element in automated email responses. While the response itself is automated, it should still feel like it was crafted with the recipient in mind. This can be achieved by using the recipient's name, referencing their specific inquiry, or including details that demonstrate an understanding of their needs. Personalization helps build rapport and trust, making the recipient feel valued and understood.

Timing is another critical factor in automated email responses. The immediacy of an automated reply can be both a strength and a weakness. While it ensures prompt communication, it can also give the impression of a lack of human involvement. To mitigate this, consider setting up a two-step process where an initial automated response acknowledges receipt of the email, followed by a more detailed reply from a human representative. This approach combines the efficiency of automation with the personal touch of human interaction.

It's also important to regularly review and update your automated email responses. As your business evolves, so too will the types of inquiries you receive. Regularly revisiting your automated responses ensures they remain relevant and accurate. This is particularly important for businesses that frequently update their products, services, or policies. An outdated response can lead to confusion and frustration, undermining the benefits of automation.

In addition to addressing specific inquiries, automated email responses can be used to enhance customer engagement. Consider incorporating elements that encourage further interaction, such as links to relevant resources, invitations to follow your social media channels, or prompts to provide feedback. These elements not only provide additional value to the recipient but also help foster a deeper connection with your audience.

While automated email responses offer numerous benefits, it's important to recognize their limitations. Not every inquiry can be addressed with a pre-written response, and some situations require a more nuanced approach. It's essential to have a system in place for identifying and escalating emails that require human intervention. This ensures that complex or sensitive issues are handled appropriately, maintaining the integrity of your communication.

The integration of automated email responses into your communication strategy should be seamless and unobtrusive. The goal is to enhance efficiency without compromising the quality of interaction. By carefully crafting responses that are personalized, timely, and relevant, you can achieve this balance, providing a positive experience for both the sender and the recipient.

In conclusion, automated email responses are a powerful tool for managing communication in a fast-paced world. By understanding your audience, crafting personalized responses, and regularly updating your content, you can harness the benefits of automation while maintaining a human touch. This approach not only improves efficiency but also strengthens relationships, fostering trust and loyalty among your audience. As you continue to refine your automated email strategy, remember that the ultimate goal is to enhance communication, making it more effective and meaningful for everyone involved.

Chatbots and Virtual Assistants

Chatbots and virtual assistants have become integral components of modern digital interactions, transforming the way businesses and individuals communicate. These tools, powered by sophisticated algorithms, are designed to simulate human conversation, providing users with instant responses and assistance. Their applications are vast, ranging from customer service and support to personal productivity and entertainment. Understanding how to effectively implement and utilize these technologies can significantly enhance user experience and operational efficiency.

The journey of chatbots and virtual assistants began with simple rule-based systems, which relied on predefined scripts to interact with users. These early iterations were limited in scope, often leading to frustration when users deviated from expected inputs. However, advancements in natural language processing and machine learning have revolutionized these tools, enabling them to understand and respond to a wide array of queries with remarkable accuracy. This evolution has paved the way for more dynamic and engaging interactions, allowing chatbots and virtual assistants to handle complex tasks and provide personalized experiences.

One of the primary benefits of chatbots and virtual assistants is their ability to provide immediate assistance. In a world where time is of the essence, users appreciate the convenience of receiving instant responses to their inquiries. This is particularly valuable in customer service, where chatbots can handle routine questions and issues, freeing up human agents to focus on more complex cases. By efficiently managing high volumes of inquiries, businesses can improve response times and customer satisfaction.

Personalization is a key factor in the success of chatbots and virtual assistants. By analyzing user data and preferences, these tools can tailor their responses to meet individual needs. This level of customization enhances user engagement, making interactions feel more relevant and meaningful. For instance, a virtual assistant might suggest personalized recommendations based on a user's previous interactions or preferences, creating a more seamless and enjoyable experience.

The integration of chatbots and virtual assistants into various platforms has also expanded their utility. From websites and mobile apps to messaging platforms and smart devices, these tools are accessible across multiple channels, providing users with consistent support wherever they are. This omnichannel presence ensures that users can interact with chatbots and virtual assistants in the manner that best suits their needs, whether through text, voice, or even visual interfaces.

Despite their many advantages, chatbots and virtual assistants are not without challenges. One of the primary concerns is ensuring that these tools can accurately understand and interpret user inputs. Misinterpretations can lead to frustration and dissatisfaction, undermining the benefits of automation. To address this, continuous training and refinement of algorithms are essential, allowing chatbots and virtual assistants to adapt to evolving language patterns and user expectations.

Another consideration is the balance between automation and human interaction. While chatbots and virtual assistants excel at handling routine tasks, there are situations where human intervention is necessary. It's important to have a system in place for escalating complex or sensitive issues to human agents, ensuring that users receive the appropriate level of support. This hybrid approach combines the efficiency of automation with the empathy and understanding of human interaction.

Security and privacy are also critical factors in the deployment of chatbots and virtual assistants. As these tools often handle sensitive information, it's essential to implement robust security measures to protect user data. This includes encryption, authentication, and compliance with data protection regulations. By prioritizing security and privacy, businesses can build trust with their users, fostering long-term relationships and loyalty.

The future of chatbots and virtual assistants is promising, with ongoing advancements in technology poised to further enhance their capabilities. As these tools become more sophisticated, they will continue to play an increasingly important role in digital interactions, offering new opportunities for innovation and growth. By staying informed about the latest developments and best practices, businesses and individuals can harness the full potential of chatbots and virtual assistants, transforming the way they communicate and operate.

In summary, chatbots and virtual assistants are powerful tools that offer numerous benefits, from improved efficiency and personalization to enhanced user engagement and satisfaction. By understanding their capabilities and limitations, and by implementing them thoughtfully and strategically, businesses and individuals can unlock their full potential, creating more meaningful and effective interactions in the digital age.

Collaborative Platforms

Collaborative platforms have emerged as essential tools in the modern workplace, revolutionizing the way teams communicate, share information, and work together. These platforms provide a digital space where individuals can collaborate in real-time, regardless of their physical location. By facilitating seamless interaction and information exchange, they have become indispensable in fostering productivity and innovation.

The rise of collaborative platforms can be traced back to the increasing need for remote work solutions and the globalization of business operations. As organizations expand their reach across borders, the demand for efficient communication tools has grown exponentially. Collaborative platforms address this need by offering a centralized hub where team members can connect, collaborate, and contribute to projects without the constraints of time zones or geographical barriers.

One of the most significant advantages of collaborative platforms is their ability to enhance communication. Traditional methods of communication, such as email, often lead to delays and misunderstandings. In contrast, collaborative platforms offer instant messaging, video conferencing, and file-sharing capabilities, enabling teams to communicate more effectively and make decisions faster. This real-time interaction fosters a sense of immediacy and engagement, allowing team members to stay connected and informed.

Moreover, collaborative platforms promote transparency and accountability within teams. By providing a shared space for project management and documentation, these tools ensure that everyone has access to the same information. This transparency helps prevent miscommunication and ensures that all team members are aligned with project goals and timelines. Additionally, the ability to track changes and updates in real-time holds individuals accountable for their contributions, encouraging a culture of responsibility and ownership.

Another key benefit of collaborative platforms is their capacity to streamline workflows and improve efficiency. By integrating various tools and applications, these platforms create a cohesive ecosystem where tasks can be managed and executed seamlessly. For instance, project management features allow teams to assign tasks, set deadlines, and monitor progress, ensuring that projects stay on track. This integration reduces the need for multiple applications and minimizes the risk of information silos, ultimately enhancing productivity.

Collaborative platforms also play a crucial role in fostering creativity and innovation. By bringing together diverse perspectives and expertise, these tools create an environment where ideas can be freely exchanged and developed. Brainstorming sessions, for example, can be conducted virtually, allowing team members to contribute their insights and feedback in real-time. This collaborative approach encourages experimentation and problem-solving, leading to more innovative solutions and outcomes.

Despite their many advantages, the successful implementation of collaborative platforms requires careful consideration and planning. One of the primary challenges is ensuring user adoption and engagement. To maximize the benefits of these tools, organizations must provide adequate training and support to help team members navigate and utilize the platform effectively. This includes offering tutorials, resources, and ongoing assistance to address any technical issues or concerns.

Security and privacy are also critical considerations when implementing collaborative platforms. As these tools often handle sensitive information, it's essential to implement robust security measures to protect data and ensure compliance with regulations. This includes encryption, access controls, and regular security audits to safeguard against potential threats and vulnerabilities.

Furthermore, organizations must be mindful of the potential for information overload. With the constant flow of communication and updates, it's easy for team members to become overwhelmed and distracted. To mitigate this, it's important to establish clear guidelines and protocols for communication and information sharing. This includes setting boundaries for notifications, prioritizing tasks, and encouraging focused work periods to maintain productivity and focus.

The future of collaborative platforms is promising, with ongoing advancements in technology poised to further enhance their capabilities. As these tools become more sophisticated, they will continue to play an increasingly important role in the workplace, offering new opportunities for innovation and growth. By staying informed about the latest developments and best practices, organizations can harness the full potential of collaborative platforms, transforming the way they work and achieve their goals.

In essence, collaborative platforms are powerful tools that offer numerous benefits, from improved communication and transparency to enhanced productivity and innovation. By understanding their capabilities and limitations, and by implementing them thoughtfully and strategically, organizations can unlock their full potential, creating more meaningful and effective collaborations in the digital age.

Video Conferencing Solutions

Video conferencing solutions have become an integral part of modern communication, transforming the way individuals and organizations interact across distances. As the world becomes increasingly interconnected, the demand for efficient and reliable video conferencing tools has surged, driven by the need for seamless communication in both professional and personal contexts. These solutions offer a dynamic platform for real-time interaction, bridging the gap between physical locations and enabling face-to-face communication without the need for travel.

The evolution of video conferencing technology can be traced back to the early days of telecommunication, but it has only recently gained widespread adoption due to advancements in internet connectivity and digital infrastructure. Today, video conferencing solutions are accessible to anyone with a stable internet connection and a compatible device, making them a versatile tool for a wide range of applications. From business meetings and virtual classrooms to social gatherings and telehealth consultations, video conferencing has become a staple in our daily lives.

One of the primary benefits of video conferencing solutions is their ability to facilitate effective communication and collaboration. Unlike traditional phone calls or emails, video conferencing allows participants to engage in face-to-face conversations, capturing non-verbal cues such as facial expressions and body language. This visual element enhances understanding and rapport, leading to more meaningful interactions and stronger relationships. Additionally, video conferencing solutions often include features such as screen sharing, virtual whiteboards, and file sharing, enabling participants to collaborate on projects and presentations in real-time.

For businesses, video conferencing solutions offer a cost-effective alternative to in-person meetings and travel. By reducing the need for physical travel, organizations can save on expenses related to transportation, accommodation, and venue rentals. This not only results in significant cost savings but also contributes to a more sustainable and environmentally friendly approach to business operations. Furthermore, video conferencing allows companies to connect with clients, partners, and employees across the globe, expanding their reach and fostering a more inclusive and diverse work environment.

In the realm of education, video conferencing solutions have revolutionized the way knowledge is delivered and consumed. Virtual classrooms and online courses have become increasingly popular, providing students with access to quality education regardless of their geographical location. Educators can leverage video conferencing tools to conduct live lectures, facilitate group discussions, and provide personalized feedback, creating an interactive and engaging learning experience. This flexibility is particularly beneficial for students in remote or underserved areas, who may otherwise have limited access to educational resources.

Telehealth is another area where video conferencing solutions have made a significant impact. By enabling remote consultations between healthcare providers and patients, video conferencing has improved access to medical care, particularly for individuals in rural or isolated communities. Patients can receive timely diagnoses and treatment recommendations without the need to travel long distances, reducing the burden on healthcare facilities and minimizing the risk of exposure to contagious diseases. Additionally, video conferencing allows healthcare professionals to collaborate and share expertise, enhancing the quality of care provided to patients.

Despite their many advantages, video conferencing solutions are not without challenges. One of the primary concerns is ensuring the security and privacy of virtual meetings. As these platforms often handle sensitive information, it is crucial to implement robust security measures to protect against unauthorized access and data breaches. This includes using encryption, secure login credentials, and regular software updates to safeguard against potential threats. Users should also be mindful of their surroundings and avoid sharing confidential information in public or unsecured locations.

Another challenge is the potential for technical difficulties, such as poor internet connectivity, audio or video lag, and compatibility issues. To mitigate these challenges, it is important to conduct regular tests and updates to ensure that the video conferencing software and hardware are functioning optimally. Users should also familiarize themselves with the platform's features and settings, enabling them to troubleshoot common issues and enhance the overall experience.

To maximize the effectiveness of video conferencing solutions, it is essential to establish clear guidelines and best practices for virtual meetings. This includes setting an agenda, establishing ground rules for participation, and ensuring that all participants have access to the necessary technology and resources. Additionally, it is important to foster an inclusive and respectful environment, encouraging active participation and engagement from all attendees.

The future of video conferencing solutions is promising, with ongoing advancements in technology poised to further enhance their capabilities. As these tools become more sophisticated, they will continue to play an increasingly important role in our personal and professional lives, offering new opportunities for connection and collaboration. By staying informed about the latest developments and best practices, individuals and organizations can harness the full potential of video conferencing solutions, transforming the way they communicate and interact in the digital age.

In essence, video conferencing solutions are powerful tools that offer numerous benefits, from enhanced communication and collaboration to cost savings and increased accessibility. By understanding their capabilities and limitations, and by implementing them thoughtfully and strategically, individuals and organizations can unlock their full potential, creating more meaningful and effective interactions in the digital age.

www.ingramcontent.com/pod-product-compliance
Lightning Source LLC
Chambersburg PA
CBHW071226130726
47998CB00002B/845